LEARN

MENTAL HEALTH TIPS

AT HOME

By Lotfi Anuar

First Edition 2020

Product Description

Learn Mental Health Tips at Home is an eBook full of information and tips how to handle symptoms of mental illness. It is written creatively in a non-academic style so that it is easily understandable to everyone. It will change the way you see yourself and others. This
eBook will give you tips to:

Achieve a healthy sleep
Overcome depression
Understand auditory hallucination
Avoid suicidal behavior and thought
Identify and help individual with deliberate self-harm
Manage aggressive behavior
Understand Obsessive Compulsive Disorder
Understand Social Anxiety Disorder
Manage Performance Anxiety
Taking care of dementia patient

The stories are personal experience of the author in treating patients for more than twenty years. The pictures and names used are not attribute to any real situation. Enjoy your readings.

TABLE OF CONTENTS

INSOMNIA

<u>Why am I having trouble to fall asleep at night?</u>

Sleep is a blessing from the God who created the cycle of Day and Night. It is naturally controlled by a part of the brain called suprachiasmatic nuclei (SCN) through the process of sleep-and-awake known as circadian rhythm. It functions through the stimulus of sunlight that enters the pupil.

This cycle is responsible to ensure that our mental capacity is at the optimum level throughout the day. For instance, we usually feel fresh and energetic at 9-11 am and have difficulties to sleep at 9-11 pm. But at 3-5 am, we will feel extremely tired and sleepy. This is the reason of why accidents frequently occur during late night and early in the morning.

Individuals affected by insomnia usually will have trouble to sleep soundly even though they are given enough time to sleep. There are some cases where they could not sleep at all, which later then makes them feel fatigue, light-headed, and hot-tempered. These conditions will affect their cognitive functions to carry out tasks on the next day.

Insomnia occurs frequently among 30 to 50 percent human population and the main contributing factor to this problem is stress. Stress can be caused by many factors such as heavy workload, breaking up in a relationship, financial and familial problems, or anxiety towards examinations. Overthinking can cause a person to feel sleepy even if they had enough sleep during the previous night.

Insomnia occurs in three stages:

1) Having difficulties to start sleeping.
2) Frequently awake in the middle of the night.
3) Short sleeping times where the person wakes up too early then they should and could not continue to sleep afterwards.

Insomnia caused by stress will go away if the cause of the stress can be solved. However, if the person cannot overcome the stress properly, it will cause depression and problems like the third stage.

TREATMENT

The main treatment for the symptoms of insomnia caused by stress is through the practice of healthy sleep discipline. Stress must be handled well through breathing exercise, progressive muscle relaxation and mind relaxation technique. In addition, spiritual and religious methods can also help to treat insomnia. Chronic insomnia can be treated through medications from the sedative and hypnotic groups such as benzodiazepine and zolpidem. Melatonin hormone treatment can also be used. The doctor will evaluate for the possibilities of others illness such as depression or anxiety that may require further treatment from the specialists.

TIPS TO ACHIEVE A HEALTHY SLEEP

1) Create a sleep schedule and avoid sleeping during the day. Go to sleep and awake according to the schedule will help to control and improve the sleep-awake cycle. Sleep when you begin to feel drowsy and do not oversleep.

2) Do not consume any forms of stimulants such as tea, coffee, alcohol or smoke cigarette before sleep. Do not sleep with an empty stomach.

3) Your bedroom should be the only place where you sleep. Decorate your bedroom and make sure your bed is always tidy. Spend some money to buy a nice comforter and an air conditioning unit. Create a warm and cozy atmosphere by placing flowers, arts, photo frames or aromatherapy candles to make you feel relaxed and comfortable.

4) Do not use your bedroom as a place to eat, watch television, or do office work. Have a mindset that bedroom should only functions as a place where you sleep. Switch off the lights and avoid any sound disturbances. If you are into reading, make sure the material that you read is something that is light and easy, and not scary.

5) Exercise regularly to build a healthy mind but do not exercise at night. It will cause your heart rate and blood pressure to increase and it will take time for both to return to normal before you sleep

6) Try to do something relaxing to ease your stress. You can play with your child at home, watch television,

hang out with friends after work to have someone to
talk to or get useful advice.

DEPRESSION

Am I suffering from depression?

Two out of ten people had experienced depression at one point of their life. The difference is, did they recover spontaneously (self-healing) or went through a professional treatment?

For those unlucky individuals, this illness will slowly take away the smiles on their face and seize their quality of life. Not to mention that there are some individuals whom their depression level is so severe that they decided to physically hurt themselves or even commit suicide.

Depression negatively affects the functions of mind and body. Depression can cause a person to feel empty and useless. They are not able to feel the sense of enjoyment when making things or doing activities that used to make them feel happy.

Appetite is also affected and so do sleep patterns. Patients will easily get irritated always look restless as they always thinking of negative thoughts. For professional workers, they will appear lethargic during the day and could not focus on their tasks.

If you are having symptoms mentioned above, do not wait for a long time to seek for treatment, and do not expect your illness to heal by itself. It may take years or not even healed at all, and you do not want to miss out on reaching your life goals.

HOW TO SEEK HELP FOR TREATMENT?

To take the first step in seeking for help is not as easy as admitting that you are having the signs of depression. This is because patients tend to isolate themselves. Furthermore, they always feel low about themselves and cannot remember when was the last time that they feel happy.

However, it is worth to get a treatment because it can help the patient to think clearly and enables them to immediately go to work as usual.

Doctors will evaluate the signs of depression and how far the illness will take a toll on the patients' life. Diagnosis will be given, and a detailed treatment plan will be explained.

During the consultation session, multiple methods of treatment will be discussed. Usually, the doctors recommend the best treatment plan for the patients. For now, the best treatment method is through the combination of medications and psychological therapy.

The healing effects can be seen from the second to the sixth week. Energy from the body and sleep patterns will be healed first before depression and suicidal thoughts are fully gone from the patients' mind. It is certainly faster comparing to lock yourself in your house for years, hoping the illness gone by itself, if possible.

Psychological therapy and counselling sessions will be conducted after the medication effects begin to show positive results. Patients will only be admitted to wards if their condition is seen as harmful to themselves or to others. For instance, if the patients hear voices in their head, delusional or having high levels of suicidal tendencies.

There are also patients who can potentially harm other people such as newborn babies or small children at home. These kinds of patients also will be admitted to the ward as well.

HOW TO OVERCOME DEPRESSION?

1. Apart from professional help, there are also other methods that can be done to brighten up your life.
2. Taking care of your health can maximize the chances to have a happy life. This includes practicing healthy lifestyles such as maintaining good sleep schedule and balanced diet intake.
3. Exercise regularly. Even though patients tend to look lethargic, exercising can stimulate the secretion of endorphins (happy hormones) that will make them feel relaxed and energetic.
4. Do creative activities that can make you feel relaxed such as drawing, writing and gardening. It can relax your mind and makes you feel satisfied.
5. Contact your friends, relatives or someone that can help you to brighten up your mood. You can make phone calls or hangout at the coffee shop. At least it can help you to connect with someone trusted rather than locking up yourself at home.

In short, if you think that you are suffering from depression, please seek professional help. There are many patients who have successfully healed from depression with treatment. They will become more concern towards their needs and much stronger in dealing with new challenges.

AUDITORY HALLUCINATION

Why am I hearing voices in my head?

Some people consider that hearing voices in their head are related to the supernatural and mystic powers. The truth is, it can occur in any illness when the chemical balance in the brain called neurotransmitter is negatively affected.

For instance, when someone is taking drugs, he too can listen to these supernatural voices and even reply to that voice. When you asked these group of people "are you hearing voices in your head today?", don't be surprised when they replied "yes".

These supernatural voices are a symptom of mental illness called "auditory hallucination". It is a type of auditory hallucination where the patients can hear the mystic voices in the form of whispers or conversation when there are literally no one talking to them.

These voices are caused by the imbalance of the neurotransmitters in the brain called dopamine. Therefore, it is not caused by ghosts or other paranormal beings as this illness can happen to anyone. During the old age, people with the ability to hear such voices were considered as a gifted but in modern medicine, it is considered as a mental illness.

Hearing supernatural voices is not a pleasant experience at all. Those who heard the voices for the first time will usually get confused and will try to look for the source of the voice. This is because they can clearly listen to the voices as if someone is speaking next to their ears.

They will try to act normally at first but later will begin to feel disturbed because not all the voices heard are nice.

TYPES OF AUDITORY HALLUCINATION

The types of auditory hallucination depend on the content and the type of mental illness faced by the patients.

For patients who suffers from depression, they will usually hear voices that lowers their self-esteem and makes them feel sad. For instance, "you are pathetic and useless!" or "your boyfriend left you because you are ugly!"

Schizophrenic patients usually will hear voices that is even more irritating such as hearing a group of non-existent humans that criticizing whatever the patient is currently doing. For instance, when the patient is taking a shower, they will listen to voices that mocking the patient's physical appearance and then laughs.

There are also patients that can listen to their inner thoughts and perceive that those inner thoughts are being spoken through a loudspeaker.

Bipolar manic patients will hear the supernatural voices praising them by saying that they are a gifted or special. For instance, they claimed that they had heard the voice of God saying that they are the descendant of a warrior who can cure illness or something along the line.

Now imagine if you had to experience the same thing in your daily life, you too will become stressed or live in fear and anxiety.

Finally, the patients will always appear pensive. They have become strayed from the reality when they begin to interact with the voices. Sometimes they argue with the voices and later will try to reply to the voices in secret. Then, they will be seen as talking to themselves and when being asked to whom they are talking to, they deny it.

TREATMENT

Patients should be treated immediately to avoid the problem from getting worst. If the disturbance left untreated, the patient would begin to show weird and eccentric behavior. They will talk, laugh, sing, smile and get angry by themselves even in public places.

At this point, people around the patient will realize that the patient should be sent for treatment. Admission to ward is necessary if the patient listens to the supernatural voices that instruct them to do something bad. For instance, the voices may instruct the patient to commit suicide or to commit a murder.

Treatment are based on the type of illness. Anti-psychotic drugs such as haloperidol, risperidone and asenapine can be used to make the voices go away. Anti-depressants will be prescribed to depressed patients. Electroconvulsive therapy and cognitive behavior therapy can also help.

Mental illness is just the same as other medical illness. It can be treated if the patients are sent to the hospital to get proper treatment.

SUICIDE

How could I have suicidal thoughts?

The urge to commit suicide is considered as a last resort when someone has given up on life. For them, death is the only way to escape from the problems that they are facing.

There are many reasons of why people are having the urge to commit suicide. One of the main reasons is related to relationship problems such as breaking up or family arguments. Almost half of them suffers from depression. There are suicide cases that are caused by other mental illness such as drug addiction, gambling, bipolar disorder and schizophrenia.

Suicide risk is higher among victims aged below 35 years old. Research have shown that women has three times more potential to commit suicide but usually the men are the ones who successful commit the suicide. Suicide cases among the elderly people are usually caused by disability due to prolonged physical pain, loneliness and depression.

EARLY SIGNS

Most victims did not make the decision to commit suicide within a day. If it is happening to a friend, you will surely notice some early signs. Do not take those signs lightly because you may be able to save your friend.

The easiest signs to be noticed is behavioral changes due to depression. Victims usually look unhappy and sometimes try to isolate themselves from the public. They may voice their feelings of hate towards themselves.

They also may indirectly leave some form of 'wills' by giving their most valuable or treasured belongings to other people or make rearrangements of personal financial matters. This usually happens because the victim does not want his family to be burdened by the cost of funeral or outstanding bills after their death. Because of that, suicide notes can usually be found together with the victim after they have committed suicide.

TIPS TO AVOID SUICIDAL BEHAVIOR AND THOUGHTS.

If you are facing the situation mentioned above, do not hesitate to ask your friend, "are you really sure that you want to commit suicide?". Ask that question and take note of his response.

If the answer is "yes", get immediate help. Look around if there is an easy way for your friend to commit suicide and try to divert his sight from looking at the hazards. It can be sharp objects, poison, or high places where your friend can jump. Do not leave the victim alone and try to coax him to go to the hospital. If all those attempts failed, try to get the attention from other people to call the police.

Check whether your friend is under the influence of drugs or alcohol. If you think that your friend has consumed something lethal, ask what kind of poison he consumed, and the amount taken. This information may be helpful during the treatment in hospital.

Be careful of what you say when you talk to your friend. There are some things that you should not say because your friend might have different interpretations and will continue to attempt suicide. You really do not want to see that right in front your eyes. This is because during that time, victims are no longer able to think like a sane person.

For instance, do not tell them that there are more unfortunate people in this world. Remember, the victim is not that stupid. They are only in severe stage of depression and still aware that there are people starving in Africa and dead soldiers in wars. This will make them to think that the world is a cruel place to be and make them even more depressed.

The same goes when you say "committing suicide is considered as a major sin. You will surely go to hell". Do remember if the victim is a non-believer, will he trust your words? But if the victim is a religious person, then his suffering must be so unbearable to him to the extent that he considers committing suicide even though he is aware of the outcome.

No sane person would want to commit suicide, but depression will take away the sanity of an individual. These kinds of individuals are hard to predict and will do anything that a normal person would not want to.

INFLICTING SELF-HARM

<u>How can someone physically hurt themselves?</u>

I was visited by a nice young girl during a professional treatment in a clinic. She looks like a nice person but a little bit shy. Her eyes were fixated on the wall, as if something is not right. She remained silent.

The referral letter stated that the teenager is suffering from severe emotional distress. I tried to ask some questions but failed. That is, until I look at her arms that is full of scars from self-injury inflicted by razor blade. Most of the cut marks looks new but some had left deep scar on the skin.

This is an example of deliberate self-harm that usually occurs to teenagers. It can happen as early as 12 years old. Many well-known individuals admitted that they have done the same thing during their teenage years. For this young girl, there must be a story behind her actions.

Slashing arm with sharp objects is one of the popular methods of self-inflicting injury. Other examples are burning own fingers, banging head, punching the walls or other methods that can cause injury and pain to the body. In extreme cases, some are willing to break their legs or hands.

Most of them mentioned that the reason of their harmful actions is to release their stress or disappointment. They feel relieved when see their own blood oozing out from their body. The truth is, they purposely injure themselves to divert their attention from emotional pain.

It is quite disappointing when query the reason of their stress is due to lack of parental guidance in overcoming daily problems such as relationship problems or family arguments. Even more unfortunate that some of the affected patients are considered too young to think about such problems.

Some of them even commit self-harm to gain attention from someone. When they failed to gain the attention that they expected at, they will try something that is more dangerous and life threatening. They actually did not mean to commit suicide, but in some unlucky cases, their actions could lead to death.

TIPS TO IDENTIFY THESE KIND OF INDIVIDUALS AND HOW TO HELP THEM.

Learn to identify the signs of self-harm so that you can be able to identify the individual at risk. This is because these individuals commit self-injury secretly. They are afraid that the public know their weaknesses. These are the signs that you can identify to those individuals:

1) They have injury marks such as cuts, scratches, scars and bruises on uncommon parts of their body.
2) They give illogical reasons when being asked about the cause of their injuries such as being involved in a road traffic accident or being scratched by a cat.
3) The try to conceal the mark of the injury with excessive clothing or make up.

4) Their emotions change abruptly and frequently. They tend to look sad and depressed but when someone noticed their behavior, they immediately try to act like a happy and normal person
5) They tend to isolate themselves from the society and prefers to be alone, away from joining activities with families and society.
6) They possess low study or work performance, lethargic and always look down on themselves.
7) They show early signs of alcohol, drug, cigarettes and psychotropic addiction.
8) They show harmful behaviors such as crossing the road without looking sideways or driving recklessly

Do not get surprise if you saw all the signs in your closest friends or families. Usually, closest individuals are the first ones who can detect the signs of self-harm. Do not reprimand them because you must remember that they had just reveal their deepest and darkest secret of their life. Gain their trust to know the root of their problem. As someone who are close to them, you may be able to help them to solve the problem.

If everything else fails, bring them to the doctor. They may suffer from mental illness such as borderline personality disorder, bipolar, depression or schizophrenia. They could be a possibility that they are having traumatic experiences due to sexual or emotional abuse in the past as well.

Parental control and guidance are crucial in these cases. This includes controlling their children's access to the internet. Did you know that they are websites that teaches the visitors on how to inflict self-harm? The worse thing is the 'tutorial' is so well made that it guaranties the death or injury of those interested trying their methods.

Please, help these innocent children because they are too young to decide whether to stay alive, deliberate self-harm or commit suicide.

AGGRESSIVE BEHAVIOR

How to deal with aggressive behavior?

Aggressive behavior often associated with anger. Anger is a normal reaction of human emotion but if not controlled, it can cause harm not only to that angry individuals but people around him as well.

Even though aggressive behavior is always associated with someone who suffers mental illness, it can also happen among normal people.

In the perspective of psychiatry, aggressiveness is a behavior than can cause serious physical or emotional harm to the victim. The aggressive behavior can be shown in a violent manner or through words that implies criminal threats.

CAUSES OF AGGRESSIVE BEHAVIOR

Individuals who shows aggressive behavior usually have defects in a part of their brains called prefrontal cortex. Apart from that, the chemical imbalance in the brain called the neurotransmitter and related hormonal secretion also contributes to the aggressive behavior.

For normal individuals, aggressive behavior can be triggered when their needs are not fulfilled or when they are in a life-threatening situation. Environmental factors can also contribute to aggressive behavior. For instance, car drivers who do not use the air conditioner in hot weather tend to sound the horn without a reason and shows aggressive behavior when being challenged.

Criminals and individuals who suffers from personality disorders such as anti-social or borderline personality disorder, their aggressive behavior is something that they enjoy, thus increasing the probability of them doing the same behavior repeatedly. However, the behavior will become increasingly more violent if they are under the influence of drugs and alcohol.

Drug addicts under the influence of drugs will become aggressive when they have become delusional or having beliefs that a particular individual is trying to do harm or murder them. They will feel that what they are believing is real and they will become aggressive towards that individual first. They will hallucinate and begin to hear supernatural voices that instructs them to be aggressive or murder someone.

Depressed patients usually will have negative outlook on themselves. This will cause them to feel extremely disappointed and angry which leads to aggressive behavior such as throwing tantrums, suicidal or homicidal thoughts. They are extremely sensitive to reprimands and criticisms.

Post-Traumatic Stress Disorder (PTSD) patients among soldiers who had witnessed traumatic events in the warzone will show aggressive behavior after their retirement if it is not treated properly.

HOW TO DEAL WITH AGGRESSIVE BEHAVIOR

1) Stay away from the aggressive individual. Call the police and inform the venue, the type of aggressive behavior and the weapons used.

2) Understand the stages of aggressive behavior. Every that begins must have an end. That applies to the feelings of anger and aggressiveness. The individual will become aggressive and eventually his anger will recede.

3) When you could not escape, the best thing that you can do is to take care of your safety while waiting for help.

4) Do not panic and stay vigilant, look for any kinds of potential hazardous items that the aggressive individual can use as a weapon. These items include knives, hard wooden stick and anything that is considered hazardous.

5) Maintain safe distance between you and the aggressive person. If the person is unarmed, make sure that you are out of his reach.

6) Bring them to an open space that can attract attention from the public to help the person.

7) Try to talk with the individual and ask them if there is anything that you can do to ease their anger.

8) Use short, clear and concise words in a calm manner.

9) Do not try to object, criticize or comment the things that are being discussed.

10) Try to show your empathy towards the individual

11) Do not try to do things that can make the individual startle such as shouting and do not retaliate.

12) Try to coax the individual to go to somewhere safer or ask the person to be calm.

13) Be confident that assistance will soon arrive. Police have their own ways and methods to diffuse the situation.

OBSESSIVE COMPULSIVE DISORDER

Is hesitancy a mental illness?

I have met a lady who complaint that her over-hesitancy has disrupted her daily activities including her daily prayers. Her hesitance began when she was in her teenage years, where she forgot to lock her house door and were being scolded by her mother.

Since then, this lady kept asking whether she had locked the door when she went out. Until now, her hesitancy has become much worse to the point that she is willing to go back to her house to check on the door even though she previously has reached her office. She also has to change the doorknob multiple times because she ended up breaking them when checking.

The same happens when she washes her hands or taking a shower, she will take around two to three hours each time. Even though she has washed them clean, the feeling of hesitance is so strong that she had to take shower few times. Consequently, she always late to work.

Her daily prayers are also disrupted. She took a long time for ablution and always had a doubt in mind about the numbers of *rakaat* that she had perform. She will then repeat the same prayer multiple times.

In her workplace, her employer complains that she always submitted her work late. This is happened because she always does the same tasks repeatedly. Every time she completed a task, she had a doubt about her quality of work. Then, she will delete her works and start over again.

Day by day, she has grown tired and stress. Now she decided to not perform her prayers or taking shower because of her over-hesitancy. She gets irritated easily and got fired from her workplace because she often skipping work.

This feeling of doubt or hesitancy in the psychological term is known as obsessive compulsive disorder (OCD). It is a form of mental disorder. The patient usually suffers from disruption of thoughts that causes the feeling of doubt. The thought will cause the patients to do the same things repeatedly such as hand washing, showering, checking the locks and others.

OCD patients are usually fussy when it comes to cleanliness issues. There are patients who refused to take money that have fallen to the floor, and there are those who frequently cleans their cellphone until they are damaged.

Apart from the feeling of doubt, the patient can be haunted by guilt or imagining things. For instance, there are patients who are haunted by guilt because they imagine themselves doing absurd dirty things such as defecating or having sexual intercourse in a house of worship even though they did not do those things in real life.

It is estimated that one of fifty people in the United States are diagnosed with OCT. This numbers are expected to be higher because the statistics given does not include individuals who do not seek for formal treatment.

Surrounding people can also be a victim. In a workplace environment, subordinates will be the objects of obsession. The tasks given must be done repeatedly even though the task has been perfected. The layout of the office cannot be changed even for an inch and every tiny mistake will cause anger.

The staff are imposed with absurd rules that is unrelated with their job scope. It is more unfortunate if they were asked to wash their hands after picking up a pen on the floor. Now, just imagine how horrible it is for the other half who live with an OCD person in the same house, for years and more to come.

TREATMENT

OCD patients knew that their actions do not make sense. They will get angry when other people say that they are uncapable of controlling their actions, when in truth, they are not able to fight the feeling of doubt.

The best way to treat OCD patients is through comprehensive approach. OCD is like depression where it is caused by low levels of neurotransmitter called serotonin in the brain. Therefore, OCD patients are also at risk of depression. The use of anti-depressants such as SSRI (for instance, fluoxetine) in high dosage can help and the effects usually can be seen after six weeks.

Patients can be sent to psychotherapy sessions to lower their sensitivity towards obsessive thoughts and compulsive acts. To improve their daily prayers, the patients are advised to get proper spiritual guide.

SOCIAL ANXIETY DISORDER

<u>Is excessive shyness normal?</u>

Miss Mary is known as someone who is quiet but not shy. She obtained good results in High School Certificate, and further her studies in one of the public universities in Kuala Lumpur in the field of mass communication.

During her studies in the University, she felt something major has happened to her. Perhaps it is not obvious before, but she started to realize that her shyness has become worse.

She startles in a situation where she becomes the center of attraction. Her face becomes red and she perspires heavily until her shirt becomes wet. Her breathing quickened and her heart beats faster. When she talks, her voice sound muffled, and she stutters a lot.

Because of that, she always skipped the first day of class to avoid introducing herself in front of lecturers and friends. Her friends will avoid from being in the same group with her to avoid getting low marks in group presentation.

She becomes depressed because she was a bright student before. This situation was never happened in the secondary school because she does not have to do presentations and most of the lessons given through spoon feeding.

This is a common example of someone who suffers from extreme shyness, in fact it is an illness called social anxiety disorder. Many people are aware of this problem, but they did not know what to do.

CONSEQUENCES

Social anxiety disorder is not something that you can take lightly because it can cause psychosocial dysfunction.

People who suffers from this disorder will not be able to enjoy life with their couple or function well in the society. They will always avoid social activities or being in the public.

Imagine a father who do not want to attend his daughter's convocation ceremony or accompany his wife to a family day gathering just because he does not want to make acquaintances with new people. They will give petty excuses and always fight to avoid themselves from joining the activities.

Friends will misunderstand the behavior and feels that the person is arrogant. In the workplace, the sufferer will feel isolated and always missed the chance for promotion. There will be no invitation of lunch breaks with coworkers, or golf playing invitation with the boss.

In workplace, they will avoid from doing presentations or attending the customers. If they are being pushed to do so, they will skip work without having second thoughts. They will frequently change their workplaces to find a new job that is suitable for their needs. They also have poor leadership skills and finally, have to do job that is not suitable or lower than their qualifications.

TREATMENT

If left untreated, it will cause a condition called agoraphobia. It is a condition where someone will try to avoid from being in a place with a lot of people such as going to weddings or go out to buy groceries at the supermarket. They are like imprisoned in their own house.

If you or someone you know suffers from this problem, take note that it is an illness and it can be treated. Do not wait until this illness destroy your career development or interpersonal relationship with others.

If the symptoms are mild, several sessions of counseling or psychotherapy are enough. However, if the symptoms are severe to the point that the person is depressed, the medications are needed.

Taking medications does not mean that someone is crazy or mentally unstable, but it shows that the person is able to make wise decision in determining what is good for himself and loved ones.

PERFORMANCE ANXIETY DISORDER

Why do I feel nervous when doing presentation or performing on stage?

MJ is a globally known and popular K-pop singer. Behind her spectacular performance, no one knows how nervous she was before performing on stage.

A month before concert, MJ already have problems to fall asleep. She worried that she could not give her best performance on stage as hoped by the fans. As the date closer, her condition has become worse. MJ perspires heavily before the performance and need to use a thick makeup. She feels nauseous, her heart beats fast and breathe heavily. MJ also have diarrhea in the morning and complaints of stomach cramps.

Her co-artist suggests MJ to consume tranquilizer pills that is sold in the black market. It helped MJ to deal with her nervousness but only for a short time because she continued to feel nervous back on the next day. MJ began to try drugs. However, the effects of the drugs cause her to become fearless. She became overreacting when performing on stage. MJ have lost her sense of shyness and always strip her clothes when singing.

Her glamorous life is full of controversy. Thankfully, MJ has a manager who is good at hiding her weaknesses. After decades, MJ lives like a drug addict. She depends on drugs and consumed tranquilizer pills every day.

One day MJ is reported dead a day before a big concert that she supposed to perform. She had a heart attack from excessive intake of drugs.

This is an example case of performance anxiety, the physical reaction when someone is feeling stressed to give their best performance. Even though there are people who have not experienced this kind of condition, but for artists, this is compulsory. They must deal with this situation multiple times throughout their career.

Performance anxiety or stage fright can also occur in other situations. For instance, it can happen to an athlete who will compete in a major tournament, a person who will go for a job interview, or a lecturer who is about to give a public lecture.

It is undeniable, that most people are having the problems of performance anxiety. The fear of giving public lectures for instance, is ranked higher than the fear towards snakes, height, or darkness for most people.

Performance anxiety is also identified as the main reason of male sexual problems. Most of them worried about their own sexual performance. Some of them are worried about the size of their genitals especially their ability to stay longer. This will encourage the use of unnecessary stimulant drugs.

Performance anxiety will hinder someone from showing their real talent. This problem should not be taken lightly as it can damages someone's career development.

Just imagine what will happen to an artist when they have to take drugs first before performing in a concert or a worker who stay unpromoted because they do not want to attend the job interview?

PREVENTION AND TREATMENT TIPS

The first step to deal with this problem is through a well preparation. For a singer, they can begin with the process of picking the songs to ease the fans. Start singing alone at home or studio before goes to pub and concert. Singing in a noisy and enthusiastic crowd is not same as singing in lounge or pub. Then, practice multiple times to improve the singing performance.

The same goes to lecturers, sportsman or those who are going for interviews. Practice will improve the level of confidence. For males who are worried about their sexual capabilities, always have a positive mind. Get advice from the professionals and do not try any kinds of stimulant drugs before consulting to a doctor.

Try to talk to yourself with positive words that can boost your morale. It is called self-talk and is suitable to be done during practice or before doing a performance. Words such as "I can do it!" can stimulate the mind to be more confident on your own abilities.

The intake of tranquilizers and stimulant drugs to eliminate the signs of fear because of performance anxiety is called as self-medicate. The placebo effect will cause more harm in the future. Before it is too late, why not get help from the specialist to get the correct treatment.

DEMENTIA

<u>Do dementia patients have ghostly or paranormal phenomenon attach to them?</u>

Taking care of a sick elderly is not an easy task. They are exposed to diseases and show many kinds of behavior.

That is the confession of Madam Ann when she tells her story of how she must take turns every three months to take care of her sick mother. During that time, her family will live in chaos, aside from the difficulties of looking for a housemaid who are willing to help.

Her mother's health deterioration began several years ago. Madam Ann found it weird when her mother gave non-sensical responses to any kinds of questions given to her. At first, she thought that her mother was having hearing problems until one day, her mother was missing in the shopping mall. Her mother was found loitering around without any purpose and could not remember where she was. She was then brought to the doctor.

The doctor has conducted some inspections and tests. The results showed that her mother is showing the signs of Alzheimer disease or dementia. This answers the question about the bizarre changes that seen in her mother all this while.

Dementia is a type of brain illness that caused by aging. It can happen to anyone as early as 65 years old. The main symptom is extreme memory loss. Other symptoms are related to the major changes in emotions and behavior.

Madam Ann remembers her experience in taking care of her mother. Her mother suffers from severe forgetfulness. She told Madam Ann that she did not had her breakfast yet, when the truth is, she had just eaten her morning meal a couple of minutes ago. She also cooked dishes that is too salty to consume because she forgets whether she has added salt in her cooking.

In the morning, Madam Ann had noticed that her mother slept and defecated at the living room because she could not find the location of the bathroom. She kept asking the same question even though she had been given the answers multiple times. She also kept walking here and there to look for items that she claimed were missing when it is stored in her personal cache. It is not surprising that Madam Ann's younger sibling prepares a special jail-like room in his house when it comes to his turn to take care of the mother.

Then, her mother started to look depressed. Her memories are affected. She could no longer remember the names of her children and her friends. When she was asked, she will get angry. She will space out when given clothes to be worn because she forgets the way to put on the clothes. She also prays at the wrong time because she could no longer differentiate between day and night.

GHOSTLY ATTACHMENT

I explained to Madam Ann that dementia patients can also experience hallucinations such as hearing supernatural voices. This is can be seen when her mother often talks to herself. Patients can also get delusional such as saying that someone is sending black magic to them, or they are being haunted by ghosts. This condition is called psychotic phenomenon.

Madam Ann took a sigh of relief. She now has solid facts to be explained to her children that their grandmother's condition was not caused by ghostly attachment. She will explain the same thing to her husband so that he would stop wasting money to go for traditional treatments from shamans who claimed that they can remove the spirit.

Research shows that dementia can cause great stress to the caretaker. Their care requires patience, commitment and high financial costs. This is the main reason why children prefer to send their old parents to the old folks' home.

If the symptoms of dementia are detected during the early stage, it can be prevented from being worse but unfortunately, the patients' memory will remain lost. However, medications such as Aricept, Exelon and Ebixa can help the patients to have a better life.

TIPS TO TAKING CARE OF DEMENTIA PATIENT

1) Avoid moving the patient from one home to another. This is to ensure that they can get use to one single home and can memorize the layout of the furniture, rooms and toilet.
2) Make sure that their room has windows so that their minds can be stimulated to identify the day and night cycle.

3) Hang a huge clock in the patient's room so that they are aware about the time changes
4) Hide car or motorcycle keys to avoid them from using the vehicle to go out from the house.
5) Teach them to memorize you phone number or supply them with notes that mentions your home address and phone numbers.
6) Equip them with mobile phones, watches or shoes that has GPS detector to allow you to track them if they went missing.

Please remain patient as these tips might be the best that you can do for them.

First Edition 20th November 2020

Written by Lotfi Anuar

Copyright Lotfi Anuar 2020

ISBN 978-967-18899-0-9

Email: lotfianuar@yahoo.com

ABOUT THE AUTHOR

Dr Lotfi Anuar is a board-certified medical doctor and Psychiatrist. He holds a Bachelor of Medicine and Bachelor of Surgery from University of Malaya, Doctor of Psychiatry from National University of Malaysia and Fellowship in Addiction Medicine from University of Malaya. Most of his studies focuses on treatment of drug addiction and stress management. He was a regular columnist in Malaysian local newspaper and wrote a lot about mental health promotion.